Elvina M Corbould

The lady's knitting-book

Containing four dozen patterns

Elvina M Corbould

The lady's knitting-book
Containing four dozen patterns

ISBN/EAN: 9783742834096

Manufactured in Europe, USA, Canada, Australia, Japa

Cover: Foto ©Thomas Meinert / pixelio.de

Manufactured and distributed by brebook publishing software
(www.brebook.com)

Elvina M Corbould

The lady's knitting-book

THE
LADY'S KNITTING - BOOK.

SECOND SERIES.

CONTAINING FOUR DOZEN PATTERNS.

BY

E. M. C.

AUTHOR OF

'THE LADY'S CROCHET-BOOK.'	FOUR SERIES.
'THE LADY'S NETTING-BOOK.'	ONE SERIES.
'THE LADY'S WORK-BOOK.'	TWO SERIES.
'THE LADY'S KNITTING-BOOK.'	FOUR SERIES.

LONDON:

HATCHARDS, PICCADILLY.

1878.

Price 1s. ; *or in cloth,* 1s. 6d.

THE
LADY'S KNITTING-BOOK.

SECOND SERIES.

CONTENTS.

INTRODUCTION.

FRESH knitting-patterns seem always welcome; I therefore hope that the following directions may be useful to those who have found *The Lady's Knitting-Book* of any assistance.

The Germans are beautiful knitters; they generally do a fancy pattern at the tops of their stockings, or else have a doubled hem, similar to English woven ones; but theirs has a Vandyke at the top.

A German peasant-girl showed me the following way, which I transcribe for the benefit of any English ladies who may like to try it:—

Cast on the number for your stocking: it ought to be divisible by 3.

Do ten or twelve plain rounds.

Eleventh round—* knit 3 together, wool forward; repeat from *.

Twelfth round—* knit 1, wool forward, knit 1 ; repeat from *.

Turn the hem inside, and pick up the stitches with other pins.

Thirteenth round—with each stitch knit up one of the lower ones as well.

The standard of measurement for the pins is Bell's Knitting Gauge.

EXPLANATIONS.

Muff.

Steel pins No. 13, and 1 oz. of white Andalusian. For a child cast on 42 ; for a full size cast on 60.

First row—plain knitting.

Second row—knit 1, knit the 2nd stitch in the following manner : put the wool round the needle in the usual way, but instead of pulling the stitch through, let the wool hang straight down over the forefinger of the left hand ; wind the wool round the finger, put it again over the needle as though you were going to knit ; then do the same a third time, and finish working this stitch, which ought to have the appearance of 3 in 1 ; knit the 3rd stitch plainly. Continue in this manner to do 1 stitch loop-knitting and the next plain.

Do 3 plain rows, and repeat from the 1st row ; be careful in the alternate rows to do the loops into the stitch, which had none in the previous row.

When the knitting is 11½ inches long cast off, and sew the top and bottom together.

Make up the muff in the following way : either line it with silk or knitting ; if the latter, cast on in white Berlin 52 stitches, and make it with plain knitting a trifle shorter than the loop-knitting. Sew the two parts together, with 3 or 4 thicknesses of wadding between. Ribbon, with elastic run in, can be sewn round the two openings and fastened off with a bow.

Tippet or Victorine, to match the above.

For a child, cast on, with white Andalusian, 36 stitches.

Knit as in the previous pattern for 18 inches, and cast off ; double it and sew the sides together.

Sew 2 large white ornamental buttons, and elastic fastening at the throat ; add small tassels to the end.

Muff.

Another way of doing these is to do every stitch loop-knitting, with only one plain row between, using Berlin wool.

Afterwards comb the wool out until it has the appearance of fur.

Crimean Helmet.

This is a kind of cap, muffling half the face, and very comfortable for gentlemen travelling by night, gamekeepers, &c.

¼ lb. brown Berlin wool, and 4 pins, No. 8. Cast on 90 stitches, 30 on each pin.

First round—plain knitting. Then do 32 rounds of ribs, 3 plain, 3 pearl.

Thirty-fourth round—knit 39 stitches on one pin, which you leave. Go on with the other 51, still keeping the ribs even : do 32 rows (not rounds) backwards and forwards, but cast off 15 stitches at each end of the last 2 rows.

Knit the stitches left on the 3rd pin, taking up at the end of every row one stitch from the 15 which you had cast off, and knitting it together with the last stitch of each row.   Do this until all the 15 have been picked up.

Now pick up 27 stitches at each side, and knit 16 rounds. Cast off.

Stocking.

The subject of socks and stockings has been so fully explained in the first series of *The Lady's Knitting-Book*, that but little remains to be said.

The following pattern is for pins No. 17, and merino, or any very fine wool.   It is full sized.

A striped stocking can be done in the same manner, and when joining the different colours knit the first round plain.

Cast on 40 stitches on 3 pins, 120 altogether.

Knit a plain round.

Second round—make the first stitch the seam-stitch (knit it in two rounds, and pearl it in the third).   Knit 1, pearl 1, for 8 rounds.   Then do plain knitting for 4 inches.

Knit (or pearl) the seam-stitch ; knit 2.   * Pearl 1, knit 3 ; repeat from *, knit the last 2.   Go on with these ribs for the remainder of the stocking.

When eighty rows are knitted, decrease on each side of

seam-stitch. * Knit 6 rounds, and increase in the same way. Repeat from * twice more.

When 13½ inches are knitted decrease every fifth row, on each side of the seam-stitch, until you have only 84 stitches on your pins. When the stocking is 23 inches long, divide for the heel by taking 22 on each side of the seam-stitch. Knit and pearl these 45 backwards and forwards for 48 rows (not rounds). Turn the heel as follows : knit 22, then the seam-stitch, which from this time forward you cease to make. Knit 4 beyond it, knit 2 together, knit 1. Turn back, pearl 11, pearl 2 together, pearl 1. Turn, knit 12, knit 2 together, knit 1. Turn, and pearl to where you turned in the preceding row ; this you can easily perceive by the little hole formed in turning ; knit the 2 stitches together, knit 1, and turn. Continue in this manner until all the stitches are worked off.

Pick up 24 side-stitches, and do one round. Now decrease for the instep. On the right-hand side of the heel, just where the ribs leave off, you slip 1, knit 1 ; pass the slipped stitch over ; continue plain knitting, and where the ribs begin again you must knit 2 together. Reduce in this way until you have 80 stitches.

When the foot is 8 inches long, reduce for the toe ; knit the ribs, all but 3 stitches ; slip 1, knit 1, pass the slipped over, knit 2, knit 2 together. Do the same on the other side. Be sure and make the decreasings exactly opposite each other, so that the upper part and the sole may lie perfectly even. Do two rounds between each decreasing, and when the foot is 9 inches long cast off, and sew up the toe on the wrong side.

Another way of turning a heel is as follows : knit the flap as usual, but it need not in this case be so long ; do the seam-stitch (which you need not make, but plainly knit it), knit 3 beyond it, knit 2 together. Turn back, pearl 8, pearl 2 together. Turn back, knit 8, knit 2 together. Continue to work off the stitches in this way, never having more than 9. Take up the side-stitches, do 2 plain rounds, and reduce for the instep. With this kind of heel do 2 plain rounds between each decreasing. Some people merely do a straight flap and sew it up, picking up the stitches all round for the sole ; but the ridge is apt to press against the foot.

Child's Petticoat and Bodice in One.

The petticoat can be done either in knitting or crochet. For the latter begin with the body, which must, of course, always be knitted.

Cast on, with merino wool and pins No. 14, 136 stitches. Knit 4, pearl 4, for about 5 inches, or as long as the body is desired. Cast off, and knit a similar second piece. Sew together, leaving about 3 inches open for the armhole. Crochet an edging round these openings, and also round the neck.

Crochet the petticoat on to the knitting by doing first 2 treble, 2 chain, and as the petticoat gets larger, do 3 instead of 2.

The petticoat on page 47 of *The Lady's Crochet-Book*, First Series, is especially suitable ; work as there directed, and then pick up 136 stitches on one half of the petticoat for the body, as directed above. Then pick up the second half and sew together.

These bodies are so elastic that they do not require any fastening, but slip easily over the child's head.

If you prefer the entire petticoat knitted proceed as follows :—

2 oz. pink and white fingering, or Berlin wool, and ivory pins No. 10. Cast on with pink and do 1 row. The knitting can be done double or plain, whichever is preferred. (For double knitting see page 27 of first series.) Cast on 136 stitches with pink, and do 1 plain row, join the white and do 6 rows, then 4 more pink rows. The rest of the petticoat is white, except the border, which must be done in pink and sewn on afterwards. When the petticoat is long enough (about 8 inches will do), rib, 4 plain, 4 pearl, for 12 rows. Join the white merino wool ; and now you must use steel pins, No. 14. Do 4 inches of ribbed knitting, 4 plain, 4 pearl, and cast off.

Do another side in the same way and sew together, leaving an opening for the armholes. Crochet round the latter, and also round the neck. Do any kind of border you prefer.

Sleeveless Jacket.

Pins No. 9, and black Berlin or fingering.

Cast on 98 stitches. Knit 12 rows.

Thirteenth row—knit 16, wool over the needle, knit 30, wool over, knit 6, wool over, knit 30, wool over, knit 16.

The alternate rows plain.

Fifteenth row—knit 17, wool over, knit 30, wool over, knit 8, wool over, knit 30, wool over, knit 17.

Seventeenth row—knit 18, wool over, knit 30, wool over, knit 10, wool over, knit 30, wool over, knit 18.

Continue in this way for 60 rows.

For the Front, knit 60 stitches backwards and forwards for 32 rows.

Thirty-third row—cast off 5 stitches (this must be at the commencement of a row); knit the rest plain.

Thirty-fourth row—reduce for the neck by taking 2 together at the end of this row, next to the cast-off stitches. Reduce thus for 31 rows and cast off for the shoulder. Then cast off 16 stitches under the arm, and take the 66 at the back between the holes. Do 16 rows plain, then decrease for 38 rows at the end of each row for shoulder. Now cast off here for the neck. Then cast off 16 for the other arm. Take the remaining 60 stitches for the second front, and do 32 rows as on the other side. Cast off 5 for neck, and then decrease at the end of every alternate row for 32 rows.

Sew the shoulders together.

Pick up 53 stitches for the right-hand side, and do 2 plain rows. Make a button-hole every 12 stitches; thus, knit 3 together; in the next stitch put the wool 3 times round the needle; in the succeeding row knit the first part, pearl the second, knit the third part of this stitch.

Do 3 more rows and cast off.

Do the same number of rows on the opposite side, and sew buttons on. It is best to put a small piece of cloth underneath for a foundation, as the buttons are apt to pull off.

Take up the waist stitches; increase after every 4 stitches.

Second row—increase, knit to the centre, and increase again.

Repeat these increasings for six rows. Then increase 3 times in the centre. Do 4 more rows, then 6 rows in brioche knitting with much coarser pins; do no increasings now.

Cast off. Take up the stitches round the neck, decrease 5 times every alternate row for 4 rows, and do 4 rows of brioche with smaller pins. Cast off.

It brightens the jacket to make the borders with violet or blue.

Crochet round the sleeves.

These are very nice, warm presents for the poor, done in coarser wool; but as this pattern is for a slight figure more stitches had better be cast on, especially the waist must be increased.

Opera Cloak, or Sortie du Bal.

Wooden or ivory pins No. 9, and ¼ lb. white and 6 oz. scarlet Lady Betty's wool, or merino wool. If the former is used, cast on less than the given number.

With merino wool cast on in white 160 stitches. Plain knitting in stripes ; join the scarlet when your white stripe is sufficiently wide. When the knitting is 3 yards and 10 inches long cast off.

Put any border you like, either crochet or knitting, with scarlet ; but the border *on the upper part lengthways* must have the pattern on the wrong side.

When the border is finished, turn back the side which has the reversed border for several inches, to make the border come on the right side ; this is the upper part of the cloak. Now, to make the hood, fold the knitting in half, and sew the two upper edges together at 17 inches from the doubled part. Fasten a tassel at the sewing, and another tassel at the bottom of the hood. Bind the neck with ribbon, leaving ends to tie at the throat. A piece of swansdown covering the ribbon forms a pretty finish, but is not absolutely necessary.

Lady's Gauntlet.

Brown and violet Berlin, and 4 needles, No. 15.

Cast on 54 stitches with brown, and rib for about 1 inch by doing 4 plain, 2 pearl. Join the violet and work for half an inch. Join the brown and work another inch, then knit a plain row, decreasing 6 stitches.

Go on with plain knitting, and in the next round commence the thumb by making 1 stitch in the middle of the first needle. Knit 3 plain rounds.

The next round increase 2 more stitches (1 on each side of the one already made). Knit 3 plain rounds. Next, add 2 stitches again (1 on each side of the other three stitches).

Go on in this way, knitting 3 plain rows between each increasing row, until you have 19 stitches for the thumbs. Slip these 19 on a piece of wool, and in their place cast on 6 extra stitches to form the gusset.

Knit 1 plain round, then decrease at the gusset in every round by taking 2 of the stitches together until 48 are left.

Rib for the third of an inch with brown, do the same with violet, then the same with brown again, and cast off.

Take up the thumb-stitches, picking up also 6 at the gusset. Decrease at the gusset as before, rib 4 rounds of brown, 4 rounds of violet, and 4 of brown again. Cast off.

Another Pattern.

Pins No. 14 or 15.

Cast on 20 stitches in black, and knit 8 rows; join scarlet (or any other bright colour) and knit 8 rows. Continue in this manner to make stripes until the knitting is long enough to go round the hand. Sew the ends together, leaving a long hole, not less than 3 inches, for the thumb. Pick up the stitches round the top on 3 needles, and rib a little border. Pick up the stitches at the other end, and with the 4 pins rib 8 rounds alternately in either colour.

Another Pattern with a full large Cuff,

WHICH CAN ALSO BE USED FOR LONG SLEEVES GOING UP THE ARM.

Cast on as above, and proceed to work the hand in the same manner, but do not sew it up. When the piece large enough for the hand is done, pick up the stitches lengthways, and do 10 rows for the wrist in ribs of 2 plain, 2 pearl. Now use bone needles No. 7, and do 7 inches in the following stitch : wool forward, slip 1, knit 2 together, every row alike. Then do 8 rows of ribbed with pins No. 14, and cast off.

Finish off as described above ; sew up the long part, and then turn it back so that the ribbed part at the end may lie over the ribbed part at the wrist. If you intend to make sleeves instead of a gauntlet make it longer, and do the last 8 rows with the bone pins instead of the steel. These gauntlets are very comfortable for young ladies at school, who cannot always keep their hands warm, and who are generally obliged to keep at a respectful distance from the fire.

Baby's Glove.

This is quite an easy pattern ; but if a prettier kind is required knit exactly as for Boy's Glove, page 15 of Fourth Series, using 2-thread Lady Betty or Andalusian wool, and pins No. 16. The hand must, of course, be a bag ; the fingers need not be separate.

4 pins, No. 15, and one skein white Andalusian, will be required.

Cast on 40 stitches; knit 1 plain row. For 2 rounds, knit 2, pearl 2, using 4 pins.

Third round—knit 2, wool forward; knit 2 together. Repeat.

Fourth round—knit 2, pearl 2.

Fifth round—the rest of the glove is all plain knitting.

9th round—the thumb begins now. Knit 2, increase (always by working into part of the next stitch) ; knit 2, increase.

Knit 2 more rows without increasing.

Twelfth round—knit 2, increase ; knit 4, increase.

Fifteenth round—knit 2, increase ; knit 6, increase.

Remember never to increase anywhere else except at this part.

Eighteenth round—knit 2, increase ; knit 8, increase.

Twenty-first round—knit 2, increase ; knit 10, increase.

Twenty-fourth round—knit 2, increase ; knit 12, increase.

Twenty-fifth round—slip the 16 thumb stitches on a piece of wool, leaving them unknitted. Go on with the other part for 24 rounds. Then decrease every 5th stitch.

Two more plain rounds, and decrease every 4th stitch.

Two plain rounds ; decrease every 3rd stitch.

Two plain rounds, and end off, sewing together on the wrong side.

Now go on with the thumb stitches. You must have 18 stitches altogether ; to make the remainder right, pick up 2 at the join. Knit 17 rounds.

Eighteenth round—knit 2 together, knit 3.   Repeat.

Two more plain rows and end off.

Crochet a little cuff, beginning with 1 chain, 2 treble, increasing every round, and scalloping the last.

Baby's Boot.

(A QUICK PATTERN.)

Two bone pins, No. 14.   This is the least pretty of the shoes.

Cast on 20 stitches in white Andalusian, and do 2 plain rows.

Third row—wool before the needle, the rest plain.   Repeat this row until you have 30 stitches.

Thirteenth row—plain knitting.   Do 3 more plain rows.

Seventeenth row—knit plain until the last 2, which must be knitted together.

Continue to reduce in this manner until you have only 20 stitches.

Twenty-sixth row—at the end of this row cast on for the heel 9 extra stitches, the next row plain.

Twenty-eighth row—wool before the needle, the remainder plain. Repeat this row until there are 34 stitches. Do 3 plain rows.

Thirty-seventh row—knit 18 stitches, now turn and knit backwards and forwards on these 18 for 8 rows to form the toe.

Forty-third row—knit the 18, and then cast on 17 more stitches, taking the left-hand pin out; the stitches will not run down : these 17 ought to be opposite those which you have let off. Do 3 plain rows.

Forty-seventh row—knit the last 2 together at the toe. Reduce in every row until you have only 31, and cast off.

Take up the 17 loose stitches and 22 more from the other part, with steel pins, No. 15, to form the leg, making 39 in all.

First row—knit 7, * increase, knit 5. Repeat from *.

Second row—you ought now to have 44 stitches. Wool before the needle, knit 2 together. Repeat.

Third row—knit and pearl alternately for 12 rows.

Fifteenth row—pearl 2, knit 2 for 18 rows.

Now do the second row of loop knitting (see Part I.), 1 plain row, and cast off. This row can either be done in white or coloured wool, according to taste. A nice way of making a tuft for the rosette is to wind the wool about 20 times round the forefinger, then pass another piece of wool through the hole and draw up ; cut the edges.

Baby's Boot, Marguerite Pattern.

This is done in two colours, the leg white and the boot blue or pink. Double Shetland wool, and 4 pins, No. 15.

Cast on 48. Knit 3, pearl 3 for 3 rounds. Pearl 3, knit 3 for the next 3.

Seventh round—Work any of the striped patterns in Third Series for 2 inches (or you can rib the first half of the leg, and do the remainder plain knitting) ; join the blue and work 1 plain round. Now take 22 for the heel and knit in rows, not rounds. Knit 3, pearl 3, reversing every fourth row so as to match the beginning to form small squares. When 18 rows are finished take the 13th and 14th together, and proceed to turn the heel as in a stocking, taking care to reverse the squares in their proper order. Pick up 12 stitches at the side. Reduce for the instep at each side until you have 48 stitches ; this makes the squares come even. When 11 squares are done (counting 11 from the leg in front) decrease on each side for the toe every other round until you have only 30 left. You must be careful to make the decreasings exactly opposite each other at the side of the boot, so that it may lie flat and even.

Knit together on the wrong side. Crochet a scalloped edging of the same colour as the boot round the top of the sock, and run a ribbon round the ankle.

The Sock for a Child of Two Years Old, on page 18 of *The Lady's Knitting-Book*, First Series, also makes a pretty baby's boot. With Andalusian wool, cast on 50, and when the sock is finished dot it over at regular intervals with pink spots. Do this with a wool needle. Crochet a top of the same colour to the boot and put a little rosette of ribbon in front. You must, of course, make holes round the ankle for pink ribbon.

Another way is to do 4 rows of plain knitting, then 1 pearl row, 1 plain row, 1 pearl row. Afterwards only spot the plain rows. The shoes look very nice dotted with filoselle instead of wool.

Baby's Boot, Striped Pattern.

Two pins, No. 15.

Cast on 72 stitches.

First row—plain.

Second row—knit 1, wool forward, slip 1, repeat ; knit the last.

Third row—brioche. There ought to be 95 stitches, or 35 sets of brioche stitch. At the end, knit 3 together to make the number come right.

Work 9 more rows of this pattern. The entire foot being brioche, forms the stripe going up the boot.

Thirteenth row—work brioche for 16 sets (that is 48 stitches, one set of brioche containing 3 knitted stitches ; remember the stitches are counted in sets, or the pattern will go wrong), knit 2 together, knit 2, knit 2 together, knit 1, knit 2 together, pearl 1, knit 2 together. Brioche for the last 15 sets.

Fourteenth row—brioche 15 sets, knit 1, pearl 6, pearl 1, knit 2 together, brioche the last 15 sets.

Fifteenth row—brioche 15 sets, pearl 1, knit 3 together, knit 4, knit 3 together, pearl 1, knit 2 together, brioche 13 sets.

Repeat in this way, decreasing on each side of the 4 centre stitches, which must always be plain; these four are to be knitted in one row and pearled in the next. And the number of stitches on each side of them must always be perfectly even. You may sometimes find the knitting make a hole where you decrease on the left side of the front part. You can sew these up afterwards, or to avoid making them, you need only pearl 1, knit together 2, instead of doing the entire brioche set ; then in coming back after pearling the 4 centre stitches either knit or pearl, so that the evenness of the stripes may not be interrupted.

This seems rather complicated, but after one trial it will really be found quite simple.

When you have done 40 rows altogether, and have only 51 stitches, the boot part is finished. There ought to be 30 plain stitches up the instep. To make the 4 plain in the centre always come even, you will sometimes be obliged to decrease in the odd rows.

Forty-first row—plain knitting. This makes holes to go round the ancle. Do any fancy pattern for 1½ inches, then decrease by knitting 2 together about every 12 stitches, so as to have only 42. Then brioche for 20 rows, a plain row, and cast off.

Sole. Cast on 20 stitches, do 1 plain row; then increase at the end of every row until there are 36; 3 plain rows, and decrease in the same way until there are 30 again; cast off, and sew to the boot on the wrong side.

With pink Shetland, herring-bone or feather stitch, down the centre of the plain piece at instep, from the ancle to the end of it. Do a second row of the same on each side, leaving off an inch from the toe; thus the centre will be longer than the two other lines.

Round the top of the sock work with the pink Shetland and a fine bone hook 1 treble, 1 chain, miss, repeat. Work so that this may be on the wrong side of the leg, because this part is afterwards turned back to form a roll.

Second round—* 4 chain, 1 double on the 3rd chain, a treble on the 2nd, and a treble on the 1st; miss 2 loops; work 1 double with the next. This ought to form a small scallop. Work another double and repeat from *. Fasten off, turn back the crotcheted top, and with a wool needle give a slight tack to the fold here and there, to keep it in place. Plait double Berlin wool and run it in the holes round ancle, adding at each end balls made of Lady Betty wool, as described in *First Series of Lady's Work-Book*, but the rounds must be made of paper the size of a shilling.

Slipper.

Any thick wool and 2 bone needles. Charity or Alloa yarn, and pins No. 9, are suitable.

Cast on 15 stitches, and knit a strip 13 inches long.

Cast on 30 more stitches and knit 8 rows.

Now decrease by knitting 2 together at the beginning and 2 at the end of every alternate row. When 18 stitches only are left, knit 3 plain rows. Decrease as before, until 12 stitches are left. Knit 2 plain rows and cast off. This ought to be knitted rather tightly to make it firm.

Sew the end of the strips to the side of the toe, and crochet a border round in which to run elastic. Bind felt soles with braid of the same colour as the wool, and then sew on the slippers. Add a rosette of braid in front.

Opera Hood.

Two oz. white Berlin and 1 oz. blue Andalusian. Pins No. 9.

Cast on 1 stitch with the white, and increase at the beginning of every row until you have 8 ; and now you must always cast on 3 extra stitches at the commencement.

Seventh row—pearl.

Eighth row—slip the 1st stitch. * Wool before the needle, knit 2 together. Repeat from *.

Ninth row—pearl.

Tenth row—plain.

Eleventh row—plain.

Go back to the 8th row. When you have increased to 156 stitches, do 2 rows without increasings. Reduce to 115, and then cast off 3 stitches at the beginning of each row for 6 rows. This finishes the fore-part ; make a plait exactly in the middle, opposite the point, and with a wool-needle and white wool gather the other part (on each side of the plait), so that it may measure exactly 20 inches, to form the neck. Pick up for the latter 98 stitches.

First row—wool before the needle, knit 2 together, knit 1. Repeat.

Second row—wool before the needle; continue plain knitting until you come to the centre stitch; bring the wool forward. Now knit the centre stitch; then bring the wool forward again: this forms 2 increasings. Do this row 12 times. Repeat from first row of the neck part.

Twenty-fifth row—like the 1st.

Two more plain rows, and cast off.

With blue Andalusian crochet 3 rounds, of 2 treble, 2 chain.

As a border for the front part of the hood have 3 balls of white Berlin, and fill a netting-needle with the 3, using them as 1 thread. Work 3 knots into each of the holes formed by the 2 chain-stitches. This makes a full ruff round the face.

For the border of the other part do 2 rows of netting with a single Berlin thread, 1 knot into each hole.

If you are not a netter, put a border of swansdown or ribbon quilling. Run a blue ribbon round the neck, and leave strings; run another round the face, drawing it slightly. Finish off with a blue bow on the peak.

Opera Hood, Louise Shape.

Three oz. white 2-thread Lady Betty wool, and bone pins No. 7.

Cast on 527 stitches; knit 1 plain row, 1 pearl row, 1 plain row.

First row of pattern.—Remember always to knit the 1st and last stitch plainly. Knit 3, wool forward, knit 7, knit 2 together, knit 2 together again, knit 7, wool forward. Repeat.

Second row—pearl 1, wool forward, pearl 6, pearl 2 together, pearl 2 together again, pearl 6, wool forward, pearl 4.

Third row—knit 5, wool forward, knit 5, knit 2 together twice, knit 5, wool forward, knit 2.

Fourth row—knit 3, wool forward, knit 4, knit 2 together twice, knit 4, wool forward, knit 6.

Fifth row—knit 7, wool forward, knit 3, knit 2 together twice, knit 3, wool forward, knit 4.

Sixth row—pearl 5, wool forward, pearl 2, pearl 2 together twice, pearl 2, wool forward, pearl 8.

Seventh row—knit 9, wool forward, knit 1, knit 2 together twice, knit 1, wool forward, knit 6.

Eighth row—knit 7, wool forward, knit 2 together twice, wool forward, knit 10.

Repeat from 1st row. The border is now finished, and the remainder is plain knitting. Knit to the end of the 14th scallop; turn back and knit 3 scallops. Turn back, and knit

3 stitches beyond where you turned in the preceding row. Do this until all the stitches are worked off.

Fold the work in half, and sew 10 inches together at the two top edges, to form the hood. Add a tassel to the peak caused by this folding. Crochet a simple edging along the top, draw up the ends, and finish them off with large tassels.

This hood can also be used to wear over the shoulders. Tack the hood very lightly into its proper fold.

Lady's Capuchin Hood.

(FOR EVENING WEAR.)

Ivory or wooden pins No. 9. 2 oz. white merino wool, 1 oz. pink.

Cast on 382 stitches with pink; this gives 14 stitches for every pattern, and 4 over : therefore the 2 first and the 2 last stitches are always to be plain knitting.

First row—plain knitting.

Second row—* knit 1, wool forward, knit 4, knit 2 together, slip 1, knit 1, pass the slipped over, knit 4, wool forward, knit 1. Repeat from *.

Third row—This and every alternate row is to be pearled until the border is finished.

K. 2   C

Fourth row—like the 2nd.

Sixth row—knit 1, wool forward, knit 2 together, wool forward, knit 2 together, wool forward, knit 2 together, slip 1, knit 1, pass the slipped over, knit 4, thread forward, knit 1. Repeat.

Eighth row—like 6th.

Tenth row—like 2nd.

Twelfth row—knit 1, wool forward, knit 4, knit 2 together, slip 1, knit 1, pass the slipped over, wool forward, slip 1, knit 1, pass the slipped over, wool forward, slip 1, knit 1, pass the slipped over, wool forward, knit 1. Repeat.

Fourteenth row—like the 12th.

Fifteenth row.—Cast off the first 56 stitches; pearl the rest; cast off the last 56 stitches.

Sixteenth row—the remainder of the hood is plain knitting. These scallops which are cast off (4 on each side) must afterwards be sewn up the sides. Join the white wool. You must now begin to decrease; the best plan is to tie a piece of red wool at the centre scallop, and also at the 6th from each side; this divides it into three parts.

When you come to the 6th scallop, knit 2 together in the middle of it; do the same with the 12th, and also with the 6th scallop from the end.

Seventeenth row—knit 2 together; decrease at the 6th scallop by knitting the middle stitch and the stitch before it together. Always decrease in this way, in order to make the lines regular. Knit the last 2 stitches together.

Eighteenth row—decrease 3 times, as in the preceding row, not at the beginning or end.

Nineteenth row—like the 18th.

Repeat these 3 rows twice.

Twenty-sixth row—decrease between the 3rd and 4th scallops at the centre, and between the 3rd and 4th scallops from the end ; knit the first 2 and the last 2 stitches together.

Do the 17th, 18th, and 19th again.

Thirtieth row—like the 26th.

Thirty-first row—decrease in the middle of the 4th scallop, and the 4th also from the end. Never forget to decrease in the centre scallop in every row.

Thirty-second row—like the 26th.

Thirty-third row—like the 31st.

Thirty-fourth row—decrease at the beginning, at the 6th, centre, 6th from the end, and the last 2 stitches.

Thirty-fifth row— decrease at 3rd, 9th, centre ; the same the other end.

Thirty-sixth row—decrease in the 2nd, 5th, centre, 5th and 2nd from end.

Thirty-seventh row—like the 26th.

Go back to the 17th row, then decrease at the 8th scallop. When you have 130 stitches only, the cape part is finished.

Now knit 2 together, wool forward twice, slip 1, knit 1, pass the slipped over.

Do a plain row. Then * knit 2, increase, repeat from *. You ought now to have 148 stitches, but a few extra will not signify. This finishes the curtain.

First row of hood—knit to within 60 stitches of the end; turn and * knit 2, increase, repeat from * to within 60 of the end. You do not increase any more after this. Turn back, and when you get to within 60 of the end, knit off 2 stitches (the 60th and 59th), and turn. Do this every time until al the stitches are knitted off.

Knit a plain row; then knit the last 2 together. Repeat until you have reduced to one stitch; cast off.

Pick up the side-stitches to form a border for the face. With white wool knit 2, knit 2 together, wool over the needle. Repeat from *. This makes small holes, into which white elastic must afterwards be run. Join the pink wool. Increase 12 times at the peak, and do the first 8 rows. Then loop-knitting (page 42 of Part I.), to make a fluffy border. Sew up the side-edging to the cape part, and run pink ribbon round the neck; finish off the peak with a pink bow. You can, if preferable, put a ribbon quilling round the face or front part.

This is a nice fit, and very becoming. You must be careful in knitting the cape not to make it longer than the four scallops which were cast off, as the corners must have the edging put on rather full, or it will not lie flat. Two yards of ribbon will be required. Sew the ends of the elastic to the ribbon.

Baby's Hood.

This is a very simple quick pattern, suitable for a young infant, instead of the silk bonnets. (If you use bone pins No. 13, and Andalusian wool, it will fit the large wax dolls; pins No. 16 do for a small doll.)

Bone or wooden pins No. 9. $\frac{1}{2}$ oz. pink and $\frac{1}{2}$ oz. white Berlin wool, Cast on 48 stitches.

First row—* wool forward, slip 1, knit 1. Repeat from *. The remainder is all Brioche stitch.

Twelfth row—join the white, and do 34 rows. Then knit as far as the 48th stitch; turn back and knit to the 24th stitch from the end; turn back again, and this time take 3 together instead of 2 at the place where you turned in the preceding row. Turn and repeat this, until all the side-stitches are worked off; this forms the crown. Pick up the stitches on each side; make holes by knitting 1, wool over the needle, knit 2 together. Then do a plain row, and join the pink. Work a piece of 12 rows to match the beginning, and cast off.

Run ribbon-strings round the holes above the curtain, and finish off with a bow of the same at the back; turn back the front, coloured part, giving it a stitch on each side to keep it in place.

Counterpane.

(LAUREL-LEAF PATTERN.)

Strutt's knitting cotton, and pins No. 14 or 15, Bell gauge.

This quilt is made in squares, and joined afterwards in such a manner that the points of the leaves meet.

Cast on 1, thread forward at the beginning of every row. Knit 2 rows.

Fourth row—* thread forward, knit 1. Repeat from *.

Fifth row—you ought now to have 6 stitches; knit 1, pearl 3, knit 2.

Sixth row—Knit 3, thread forward, knit 1, thread forward, knit 3.

Seventh row—knit 2, pearl 5, knit 3.

Eighth row—knit 5, thread forward, knit 1, thread forward, knit 5.

Ninth row—knit 3, pearl 7, knit 4.

Tenth row—knit 7, thread forward, knit 1, thread forward, knit the rest.

Eleventh row—knit 4, pearl 9, knit 5.

Knit the twelfth row.

Thirteenth row—knit 5, pearl 9, knit the rest. Continue in this way, every time knitting 1 more, and always pearling the 9. The alternate rows plain.

Twenty-second row—knit 10, slip 1, knit 1, pass slip over, knit 5, knit 2 together, the rest plain.

Twenty-third row—knit 10, pearl 7, knit the remainder.

Twenty-fourth row—knit 11, slip 1, knit 1, pass slip over, knit 3, knit 2 together, plain.

Twenty-fifth row—knit 11, pearl 5, plain.

Twenty-sixth row—knit 12, slip 1, knit 1, pass slip over, knit 1, knit 2 together, plain.

Twenty-seventh row—knit 12, pearl 3, plain.

Twenty-eighth row—knit 13, slip 1, knit 2 together, pass slip over. This finishes the leaf. The other half of the square is in ribs, decreasing at the beginning of every row, thus : pearl 1 row, knit 1 row, pearl 1 row, knit 2 rows, pearl 1 row.

Wheat-ear Pattern.

Cast on 17 for every pattern, and 4 over. Do two plain stitches at the beginning and end of every row.

Do 4 plain rows.

First row of pattern—knit 2 together, knit 6, wool over the needle, knit 1, wool over the needle, knit 6, knit 2 together.

Second row—pearl.

Repeat these rows 3 times.

Ninth row—plain knitting.

Tenth row—pearl.

Eleventh row—knit 2 together, knit 2, wool over the needle, knit 1, wool over the needle, knit 1, slip 1, knit 1, pass the slipped over, knit 1, knit 2 together, knit 1, wool over the needle, knit 2, knit 2 together.

Twelfth row—pearl.

Repeat these 2 rows 3 times.

Nineteenth row—plain knitting.

Twentieth row—pearl.

Now go back to the first row of pattern.

Feather Pattern.

This is a very old pattern indeed ; but old friends are often the best, so I give it without apology.

It takes 25 stitches to form a pattern.

Cast on 50 or more stitches, and knit 2 plain rows.

First row of pattern—take 2 together 4 times, * wool over

the needle, 1 plain. Repeat from * 7 times more, then take 2 together 4 times, and pearl the last.

Second row—pearl.
Third row—plain.
Fourth row—plain.
Repeat from first row of pattern.

Talisman Pattern.

Twenty stitches are required for every pattern.
Do two rows of plain knitting before beginning it.
First row—pearl 8, knit 2, pearl 8, knit 2.
Second row—pearl 2, knit 8, pearl 2, knit 8.
Third row—plain knitting.
Fourth row—pearl.
Fifth row—pearl 3, knit 2, pearl 8, knit 2, pearl 5.
Sixth row—knit 5, pearl 2, knit 8, pearl 2, knit 3.
Seventh row—plain knitting.
Eighth row—plain knitting.
Go back to the first row. This is pretty for couvrettes, or for babies' boots.

Eyelet Pattern.

Cast on in sevens.

First row—thread forward, slip 1, knit 1, pass the slipped over, knit 5.

Second row—pearl.

Third row—thread forward, slip 1, knit 1, pass the slipped over, knit 1, pearl 3, knit 1.

Fourth row—pearl 1, knit 1, thread forward, knit 2 together, pearl 3.

Fifth row—thread forward, slip 1, knit 1, pass the slipped over, knit 1, pearl 3, knit 1.

Sixth row—pearl.

Seventh row—thread forward, slip 1, knit 1, pass the slipped over, knit 5.

Eighth row—pearl.

Go back to the 3rd row.

This can be made into a handsome couvrette or berceaunette by casting on the required number of stitches in white, and running narrow blue ribbon down the holes; put ribbon bows at the corners.

Lorne Pattern.

Cast on any number of stitches which can be divided by 5 and 2 over, to enable you always to knit the first and last stitches plainly.

First row.—knit 2, wool forward, knit 3 together, wool forward.

Second row—pearl 3, knit 2.

Third row—pearl 2, knit 3.

Victoria Pattern.

Cast on any number divisible by 6 and 2 over, so as to always knit the first and last stitch plainly.

First row—wool forward, slip 1, knit 2 together, pass the slipped over, wool forward, knit 3.

Second row—plain knitting.

Third row—knit 3, wool forward, slip 1, knit 2 together, pass the slipped over, wool forward.

Fourth row—plain knitting.

Zigzag Pattern.

Cast on any number divisible by 9.

First row—thread forward, knit 3, knit 2 together, knit 4.

Second row—plain knitting.

Third row—thread forward, knit 3, knit 2 together, knit 4.

Fourth row—plain knitting. Repeat from the first row.

Ninth row—knit 1, thread forward, knit 3, slip 1, knit 1, pass the slipped over, knit 3.

Tenth row—plain knitting.

Eleventh row—knit 2, thread forward, knit 3, slip 1, knit 1, pass the slipped over, knit 2.

Twelfth row—plain knitting.

Thirteenth row—knit 3, thread forward, knit 3, slip 1, knit 1, pass the slipped over, knit 1.

Fourteenth row—plain knitting.

Fifteenth row—knit 3 stitches; then begin again at the first row.

If you wish the pattern to lie more flat and even, pearl the alternate two, instead of knitting them. It makes a very good border, too : begin with—knit a row, pearl a row, knit a row; then commence the pattern, and pearl instead of knitting the intermediate rows.

Borders.

For a Shetland shawl the Feather Pattern is very pretty, and it makes a scallop at the part which is cast off. Pick up the stitches for the first side; increase at the beginning of every row until the knitting is deep enough. You must remember always to pearl or knit these extra increased stitches, and to begin the feather at the proper stitch, or it will spoil the pattern. When you have cast off the first side, pick up the stitches on the second side, and proceed in the same manner. Either knit in the increased stitches at the corner, or sew them up afterwards. When all four sides are completed, do 1 round of crochet; but should you not like that, it will do very well without.

The following is also a pretty border :—

Cast on any number of stitches in 14's, and add 2 over. Knit a row, pearl a row, knit a row.

First row of pattern—knit 1, * knit 1, thread forward, knit 4, slip 1, knit 1, pass the slipped over, knit 1, knit 2 together, knit 4, thread forward. Repeat from *. Knit the last stitch.

Second row.—This and every alternate row is pearled.

Third row—knit 1, * knit 2, thread forward, knit 3, slip 1,

knit 1, pass the slipped over, knit 1, knit 2 together, knit 3, thread forward, knit 1. Repeat from *. Knit the last stitch.

Fifth row—knit 1, * knit 3, thread forward, knit 2, slip 1, knit 1, pass the slipped over, knit 1, knit 2 together, knit 2, thread forward, knit 2. Repeat from *. Knit the last stitch.

Seventh row—knit 1, * knit 4, thread forward, knit 1, slip 1, knit 1, pass the slipped over, knit 1, knit 2 together, knit 1, thread forward, knit 3. Repeat from *. Knit the last stitch.

Ninth row—knit 1, * knit 5, thread forward, slip 1, knit 1, pass the slipped over, knit 1, knit 2 together, thread forward, knit 4. Repeat from *. Knit the last stitch.

Pearl a row, then go back to the first row.

You can run ribbon or some bright-coloured coarse wool up and down these holes; or it looks very nice plain.

Couvrette.

Pins No. 5 and double Berlin or fleecy wool. Three shades of bluish green, and brown shaded off to white, are very good contrasts; but not a vivid gas green.

Cast on 11 stitches for the first stripe.

First row—knit 3, wool forward, pearl 2 together, knit 1, pearl 2 together, wool forward, knit 3.

The intermediate rows are pearled.

Third row—knit 4, wool forward, pearl 3 together, wool forward, knit 4.

Fifth row—knit 3, pearl 2 together, wool forward, knit 1, wool forward, pearl 2 together, knit 3.

The seventh, ninth, and eleventh rows like the fifth.

Thirteenth row—knit 3, wool forward, pearl 2 together, knit 1, pearl 2 together, wool forward, knit 3.

Fifteenth row—Like the thirteenth. Repeat from the first row.

Crochet or sew the stripes together.

Turkish Penwiper.

Crimson Andalusian wool and pins No. 15.

Cast on 18 on 3 pins, making 54 altogether.

Knit a round, pearl a round, knit a round, pearl a round. The remainder in plain knitting. Do about 36 rounds; now decrease by dividing your stitches into 6 parts, and in every round knit 2 together at the commencement of each division. This forms a star of 6 points, and 6 stitches will remain on the needles. These are to be drawn up and sewn together. Attach a blue tassel to the top. The part on which the pens are wiped is done by folding in half a sufficient number of lengths of black wool to fill the cap. Tie them together in a kind of stumpy tassel, and attach to the inside top of the fez.

Cotton Quilt in Stripes.

A great many of the fancy stitches, such as Wheat-ear Pattern, and several others, make handsome counterpanes; but I advise all knitters to try over and compare the stitches, as a quilt is a serious undertaking, and it is a great pity not to feel satisfied with the labour when completed.

Baby's Boot, on Two Pins.

Ivory pins No. 13, and white Lady Betty wool.

Cast on 48 stitches, and do 18 rows of ribbed, 2 plain, 2 pearl.
* Knit a row, pearl a row. Repeat from * for 18 rows.

Thirty-seventh row—slip 1, take 2 together, continue knitting 2 together for the remainder of the row.

Thirty-eighth row—slip 1, * wool over the needle, knit 1, repeat from *.

Thirty-ninth row—knitted.

Fortieth row—slip 1, knit 2 together, knit 9, knit 2 together, knit 20, knit 2 together, knit 9, knit 2 together, knit 1.

Forty-first row—plain knitting.

Forty second row—slip 1, knit 2 together; knit the third and second from the end together. The rest plain.

Forty-third row—plain.

Forty-fifth row—knit 14, slip 15 on a piece of wool and leave unknitted, knit the last 14.

Forty-sixth row—pearl back on these 14; the pin may be taken out of the other stitches, they will not run down. Cast on 22 more stitches by the side of the 14, and continue on these 36 for 14 rows, in lengthway ribs, which are done by pearling every 8th row.

K. 2   D

Fifteenth row—slip 1, take 2 together, to form the toe; the rest plain. Pearl the next, and the seventeenth row is like the fifteenth. The alternate rows do not decrease.

Nineteenth row—Decrease at the beginning and end of this row.

Twenty-first row—Decrease twice at the beginning, and twice at the end of this row.

Twenty-third row—Like twenty-first.

The twenty-fifth and twenty-seventh rows only decrease once at the commencement or toe.

Twenty-eighth row—leave these stitches.

With another pin, pick up the 22 stitches at the beginning of this part; knit on them for the instep, making the ribs as usual. These bottom stitches must be taken up in such a manner that they look like a continuation of the rib.

Increase at the toe by picking up a stitch until you have 29. Do 4 rows, and then decrease at the toe every alternate row until you have 22 stitches again. Take up the 14 which had been left unknitted. Do 14 rows, and decrease as on the other side. Join the sole by knitting together the stitches off both pins. Sew the instep to the stitches you had slipped on the piece of wool.

With steel pins, No. 16, use 4 thread Lady Betty.

Sock for Crochet Boot.

This sock is intended for the leg of Crochet Boot on p. 40 of the *Lady's Crochet-Book*, First Series. A knitted sock is so much prettier than a crocheted one.

Finish the boot as directed in pink or any other bright colour. Pick up 18 stitches on 3 pins, altogether 54, with white merino yarn and pins No. 17. Do 1 plain round.

Second round—Wool forward, slip 1, knit 2 together, pass the slipped stitch over, bring the wool forward, knit 3.

Third round—pearl.

Fourth round,—knit 3, wool forward, slip 1, knit 2 together, pass the slipped over, bring wool forward.

Fifth round—pearl.

Go back to the second round, and continue thus until 25 rounds are finished.

Twenty-sixth round—Do the remainder in ribs of 2 and 2. When the sock is 2 inches long cast off.

Sock for Crochet Boot, on Two Pins.

White Angola wool, and pins No. 16.
Cast on 44 and knit 2 plain rows.
Fourth row—pearl 8, knit 2. Repeat.

Fifth row—pearl 2, knit 8.   Repeat.

Sixth row—plain knitting.

Seventh row—pearl.

Eighth row— pearl 3, knit 2, pearl 8, knit 2, pearl 5.

Ninth row—knit 5, pearl 2, knit 8, pearl 2, knit 3.

Tenth row—plain knitting.

Eleventh row—plain knitting.

Repeat from the fourth row.

Twentieth row—(this ought to be on the right-hand side of the knitting), knit 1, wool forward, slip 1, knit 2 together, pass the slipped over, wool forward, knit 1.

Twenty-first row—pearl.

Twenty-second row—like twentieth.

Twenty-third row—pearl.

Twenty-fourth row—knit 2 together, * wool forward, knit 1 wool forward, slip 1, knit 2 together, pass the slipped over, repeat from *.   You will not quite finish the pattern of this row.

Twenty-fifth row—pearl.

Twenty-sixth row—knit 2 together, * wool forward, knit 1, wool forward, slip 1, knit 2 together, pass the slipped over, repeat.   Knit the stitches over, plain.   Repeat from twentieth row ; when 2 inches are done cast off, and sew the boot and sock together on the wrong side.   You can crochet an edging where the two meet or not, as preferred.

Shetland Veil.

This is a rounded shape; ½ oz. white Pyrenees wool, and bone pins No. 9, will be required.

Cast on 156; always do the first and last stitch plain.

Knit a row, pearl a row, knit a row.

Fifth row—slip 1, * knit 1, put the wool over the needle, knit 4, knit 2 together, slip 1, knit 1, pass the slipped over, knit 4, wool over, knit 1. Repeat from *. Knit the last stitch.

Sixth row—pearl.

Seventh row.—Remember to knit the first plain, or the pattern will come wrong. This row is like the first.

Eighth row—knit.

Ninth row—slip 1, * knit 1, wool forward, knit 2 together, wool forward, knit 2 together, wool forward, knit 2 together, slip 1, knit 1, pass the slipped over, knit 4, wool forward, knit 1. Repeat from *.

Tenth row—pearl.

Eleventh row—like ninth.

Twelfth row—pearl.

Thirteenth row—like fifth.

Fourteenth row—knit.

Fifteenth row—slip 1, * knit 1, wool forward, knit 4, knit 2 together, slip 1, knit 1, pass the slipped over, wool forward, slip 1, knit 1, pass the slipped over, wool forward, slip 1, knit 1, pass the slipped over, wool forward, knit 1. Repeat from *.

Sixteenth row—pearl

Seventeenth row—like fifteenth.

Eighteenth row—pearl. Repeat from fifth row.

The rest of the veil is done in the following simple stitch :— Wool over the needle, knit 2 together. Every row is alike. Knit as far as the end of 7th scallop; turn back, knit 3 scallops ; turn back, and where you turned in the preceding row at the 7th scallop knit off 4 more. Continue in this way to knit off 4 more stitches every time, until all are knitted off. This finishes the veil, except the holes for the ribbon. Knit 2 together every time, and in the next row knit 1, wool over the needle. If you desire the veil larger, pick up the sides of the edge, and go on knitting as desired. Increase at the beginning of the rows.

For a square veil do any border, and some open stitch for the remainder ; you will not require so many stitches as for the round shape.

When finished, they must be damped and pinned out flat upon a clean cloth.

Baby's Gaiter, on Two Pins.

Cast on 52 stitches with Berlin wool, and bone pins No. 14.
Do 18 ribbed and 12 plain rows.

31st row—knit 2, make 1, knit 48, make 1, knit 2.

Knit 5 plain rows.

37th row—knit 2, make 1, knit all but 2 stitches, make 1, knit 2.

Knit 14 rows.

52nd row—knit 1, knit 2 together, knit 52, knit 2 together, knit 1.

* Knit 5 rows.

58th row—knit 1, take 2 together, knit all but 3, then knit 2 together, knit 1.   Repeat from * five times.

89th row—now knit 18 plain rows.

106th row—knit 13, make 1, knit 18, make 1, knit 13.

107th row—plain.

108th row—knit 13, make 1, knit 20, make 1, knit 13.

Knit two rows in this way, knitting 22 instead of 20.

111th row—knit 37, * turn and knit 24. Repeat from * twice.

You henceforth only knit the centre stitches, the rest are left unworked.

112th row—knit 2, take 2 together, knit 16, take 2 together, knit 2.

* Knit 3 rows.

116th row—knit 2, take 2 together, knit 14, take 2 together, knit 2. Repeat from * four times, knitting 2 stitches less each time in the centre.

129th row—knit 2 plain rows.

131st row—now pick up 13 stitches from one side, knit the rest of the stitches, knit back, and pick up 13 on the other side Knit 3 more rows, and cast off.

——— ———

Child's Gaiter, on Four Pins.

For a child of two, use steel pins, No. 14 (or if you use bone pins, No. 13, only cast on 57 stitches).

The next size, use bone pins, No. 13, and grey Berlin fingering wool.

Cast on 63 stitches.

Make the first stitch your seam-stitch, that is, you pearl in one round and knit it in the two succeeding rounds.

Knit 1, pearl 1 for 14 rows.

Fifteenth-round—knit 2, pearl 2, for the remainder of the gaiter.

Reduce at each side of the seam-stitch in the sixty-fourth, seventy-second, seventy-eighth, and eighty-seventh rounds.

One hundred and sixth round—knit backwards and forwards on the 13 stitches which are on each side of the seam-stitch, leaving the other 26 unknitted. When you have knitted 18 rows on the 27 stitches, cast them off. Keep the last cast off stitch on the pin, and raise 9 at the side of this straight flap, rib the front or second needle, then raise 10 more from the other side of the flap with your third needle. Pearl back on these 10, rib the 2nd needle, pearl the last 10.

Second row—knit 8, knit 2 together, rib the 2nd needle, knit 2 together, knit 8.

Third row—pearl 9, rib the centre, pearl the last 9.

Fourth row—knit 7, knit 2 together, rib the centre, knit 2 together, knit 7. Continue thus.

When the last of these plain stitches is knitted to the ribs, do 8 more rows and cast off.

Add a leather strap.

Very Close Knitting.

This is a good stitch for the hand of a gauntlet.

First row—knit 1, slip 1. Repeat.

Second row—plain.

Repeat these alternately ; the slipped stitch must always come over the slipped one in the row beneath.

Some people use this pattern for the heels and toes to stockings.

Border and Curtains.

The following pattern is also a good one for curtains. Knitted curtains are sometimes worked in stripes, with strips of muslin between.

If it is for a border, knit a row, pearl a row, knit a row. Cast on 42 stitches (it takes 21 to form the pattern).

First row—knit 3, thread forward, knit 7, knit 2 together twice, knit 7, thread forward. Repeat.

Second row—pearl 1, thread over, pearl 6, pearl 2 together twice, pearl 6, thread over, pearl 4. Repeat.

Third row—knit 5, thread forward, knit 5, knit 2 together twice, knit 5, thread forward, knit 2.

Fourth row—Pearl 3, thread over, pearl 4, pearl 2 together twice, pearl 4, thread forward, pearl 6. Repeat.

Fifth row—knit 7, thread forward, knit 3, knit 2 together, knit 3, thread forward, knit 4.

Sixth row—pearl 5, thread over, pearl 2, pearl 2 together twice, pearl 2, thread over, pearl 8.

Seventh row—knit 9, thread forward, knit 1, knit 2 together twice, knit 1, thread forward, knit 6.

Eighth row—pearl 7, thread over, pearl 2 together twice, thread over, pearl 10.

Mat.

Green Berlin wool, and pins No. 14. This can be done all in one colour, but it looks prettier in shades.

Cast on 24 stitches. The first row plain knitting.

Second row—*wool forward, knit 2 together, slip 1 ; repeat from *. The whole mat is done in this stitch, every row alike. Leave the last 3 stitches unknitted, turn back, and go on with the next row.

Fourth row—leave the last 6 unknitted, turn back, and do the fifth row.

Sixth row—leave the last 9 unknitted, and continue in this manner, 3 more every time, until you get to the end of the stitches.

Now join the next shade and knit the entire row.

The next row is like the second. This makes the round ; sew it up when finished, and put a moss fringe. One ball of shaded green wool, with 10 or 14 stitches. Knit a plain piece long enough to go round the mat, then damp it, and leave all night in an oven (not in too hot a one). Cast off 3 stitches and unravel all the rest. Then sew it round.

Another pretty border is to do loop-knitting (see Part I.), leaving 2 plain rows between the second.

Antimacassar.

Strutt's knitting cotton No. 6.

Cast on 126 stitches.

First row—knit 11, thread forward, slip 1, knit 1, pass the slipped over, knit 8.

Second and every alternate row is pearled.

Third row—knit 9, knit 2 together, thread forward, knit 1, thread forward, slip 1, knit 1, pass the slipped over, knit 7.

Fifth row—knit 8, knit 2 together, thread forward, knit 3, thread forward, slip 1, knit 1, pass the slipped over, knit 6.

Seventh row—knit 7, knit 2 together, thread forward, knit 2, thread forward, slip 1, knit 1, pass the slipped over, knit 1, thread forward, slip 1, knit 1, pass the slipped over, knit 5.

Ninth row—knit 6, knit 2 together, thread forward, knit 1, knit 2 together, thread forward, knit 1, thread forward, slip 1, knit 1, pass the slipped over, knit 1, thread forward, slip 1, knit 1, pass the slipped over, knit 4.

Eleventh row—knit 5, knit 2 together, thread forward, knit 1, knit 2 together, thread forward, knit 3, thread forward, slip 1, knit 1, pass the slipped over, knit 1, thread forward, slip 1 knit 1, pass the slipped over, knit 3.

Thirteenth row—knit 4, knit 2 together, thread forward, knit 1, knit 2 together, thread forward, knit 2, thread forward, slip 1, knit 1, pass the slipped over, knit 1, thread forward, slip 1, knit 1, pass the slipped over, knit 1, thread forward, slip 1, knit 1, pass the slipped over, knit 2.

Fifteenth row—Like the ninth.

Seventeenth row—Like the eleventh.

Nineteenth row—Like the seventh.

Twenty-first row—Like the third.

Twenty-third row.—Like the first.

Pearl the twenty-fourth row.

Twenty-fifth row—knit 19 stitches, and begin again as at the first row.

Knit the desired length and cast off. Add a fringe.

The pattern takes 21 stitches, so that if you require a smaller or a larger size you can easily calculate the amount of stitches you may want.

Pincushion.

Evans' crochet cotton No. 10, and steel pins No. 15.

Cast on 50 stitches, and do any fancy stitch until large enough. You can either make it twice as long as the size of the pincushion, so as to have both sides alike, or the back can be muslin.

Make a calico bag the same size as the cover, and stuff with bran. Cover this with crimson, or any bright-coloured silk, and slip it inside the knitting. Sew up the last side.

Crochet any simple edging round it, or sew on lace.

Infant's Vest.

Cast on 92 stitches with merino wool and pins No. 17.

Knit 12 plain at the beginning and end of every row.

The intervening 68, do 4 plain 4 pearl alternately. Knit 102 rows, then cast off all but 12 stitches. Knit 32 rows for the shoulder-strap. Do a second side in the same manner. For the gussets cast on 21, and knit 2 together at the end of each row. Sew in the gusset 20 rows from the top of the vest.

Crochet an edge round the sleeves and top thus :—1 single, 1 chain, miss 3, 2 treble, 1 chain, 2 treble in the same hole, 1 chain, miss 3, 1 single, 1 chain, miss 3, 2 treble, 1 chain, 2 treble in same hole. Repeat.

'Lady's Vest' in Part I. is also very nice for a baby. Use merino wool and pins No. 16. For a larger size, pins No. 14.

Tea Cosy.

Steel pins No. 10, ¼ lb. blue double Berlin wool.

Cast on 90 stitches.

First row—1 plain, 1 pearl. Repeat.

Every row is alike, remembering to pearl where in the pre-ceding row the stitch was knitted.

When 10 inches are done cast off, and work the other side in a similar manner.

Cut off the upper corners to the shape of a cosy. This knit-ting will not run down. It is best to have a brown-paper pattern, in order to be quite exact. Have ready a monogram, or some other design, worked in gold or yellow silk : it must be a toler-able size, or the effect will be poor-looking. You can either buy the design at a fancy shop, or, if you be an embroideress, you can easily make one in the following manner :—Trace or draw the monogram on tissue paper, tack this on the centre of the cosy, and then run, with either white or yellow thread, round every line, taking care to preserve the outline clear ; after which, tear away the paper, and embroider in satin-stitch, running silk under the thick parts as with *broderie Anglaise.*

Sew the two sides together, and finish in the usual way ; that is, line with quilted cashmere or silk ; put several thicknesses of wadding as well as the quilting, and finish off with a blue and yellow cord. It is an improvement to put a border of embroidered leaves round the margin.

Ribbing Sideways.

To make the ribs longitudinal instead of straight, bring the thread forward, take 2 together, pearl 2. Repeat.

The next row—knit 2, thread over the needle, pearl 2 together.

LONDON:
JOHN STRANGEWAYS, PRINTER,
Castle St. Leicester Sq.

www.ingramcontent.com/pod-product-compliance
Lightning Source LLC
Chambersburg PA
CBHW022022080426
42733CB00007B/687